I0789484

Garden as though you
will live forever !
William Kent

Large Flowering Flat-Pea | China-Rose Hibiscus

Date

Date:

Date

Date:

Date

Date:

Date

Date:

Date

Canary Belt-Flower / Azure Convolvulus

Date

Date:

Date

Date:

Date

Date:

Date

Date:

Date

Grass-Leaved Aristea | Silver Leav'd Crane's-Bill

Date

Date:

Date

Date:

Date

Date:

Date

Date:

Date

Date:

Date

Date:

Date

Date:

Date

Broad-Leaved Kalmia | Vernal Bulbocodium

Date

Date:

Date

Date:

Date

Date:

Date

Blue Lily | Safron Coloured Ixia

Date

Date:

Date

Date:

Date

Date:

Date

Crown Imperial | Canada Puccoon or Bloodworth

Date

Date:

Date

Date:

Date

Date:

Date

Trumpet-Flower | Winged-Podded Sophora

Date

Date:

Date

Date:

Date

Date:

Date

Dwarf Almond / Scarlet Ixora

Date

Date:

Date

Date:

Date

Date:

Date

Upright Trillium | Bearded Pink or Sweet William

Date

Date:

Date

Date:

Date

Date:

Date

Common Laburnum | Vernal Gentian

Date

Date:

Date

Date:

Date

Date:

Date

Pellitory of Spain | Common Indian Reed or Shot

Date

Date:

Date

Date:

Date

Date:

Date

Fringed Epidendrum | Garden Hydrangea

Date

Date:

Date

Date:

Date

Date:

Date

Thick-Stalked Crane-Bill | Kidney Leav'd Crane-Bill

Date

Date:

Date

Date:

Date

Date:

Date

Balm-Leaved Archangel / Great Flower'd Balm

Date

Date:

Date

Date:

Date

Date:

Date

Common Lilac | Scarlet Azalea

Date

Date:

Date

Date:

Date

Date:

Date

Golden Ornithogalum | Perennial Lupine

Date

Date:

Date

Date:

Date

Date:

Date

Glitthering Fig-Marygold | Yellow Azalea

Date

Date:

Date

Date:

Date

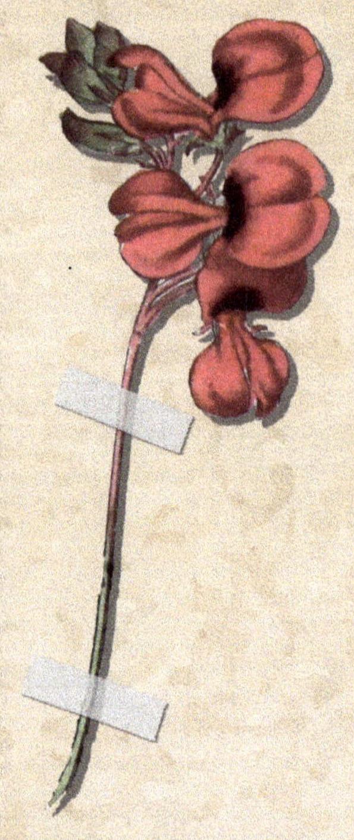

Date:

Date

Winged Lotus / Scarlet Bladder-Senna

Date

Date:

Date

Date:

Date

Date:

Date

Parrot-Beaked Heliconia | Elder-Scented Iris

Date